# ESOL Strategies for Teaching Content

## Facilitating Instruction for English Language Learners

*2001*

### Jodi Reiss
*Florida International University*
*Miami, Florida*

Merrill
Prentice Hall

Upper Saddle River, New Jersey
Columbus, Ohio

**Vice President and Publisher:** Jeffery W. Johnston
**Acquisitions Editor:** Debra A. Stollenwerk
**Editorial Assistant:** Penny S. Burleson
**Production Editor:** Kimberly J. Lundy
**Design Coordinator:** Diane C. Lorenzo
**Cover Designer:** Linda Fares
**Production Manager:** Pamela D. Bennett
**Director of Marketing:** Kevin Flanagan
**Marketing Manager:** Amy June
**Marketing Services Manager:** Krista Groshong

10 9 8 7 6 5 4 3

ISBN: 0-13-090845-2

# ACKNOWLEDGMENTS

Special thanks to the following people for their invaluable assistance with this book:

Ron Elkind, my wonderful husband, for his patience, support, and encouragement;

Ashley Reiss, my gifted and talented daughter, for her thoughtful suggestions and ideas;

Oneyda Paneque, my friend and colleague, for her wisdom and advice; and

Debbie Stollenwerk, my editor, for her vision and guidance.

# TABLE OF CONTENTS

# INTRODUCTION

This text is designed for current and future teachers of math, science, and social studies in grades three through twelve who seek ways to reach and teach the English language learners in their classrooms. It is filled not with generalities about what the perfect teacher should know and do, but with detailed advice, suggestions, and guidelines of a very practical and applied nature for teachers who would like to *learn* what they need to know and do. My goal is to present an organized and clearly written guide to facilitating comprehension of content for the students in your classes who are in the process of learning the English language.

I would like to explain why I chose to use the terms *ESOL students* and *English language learners* throughout this book. As you will see in the Glossary of Acronyms included at the end, there are many choices of terminology.

I used the term *ESOL—English for Speakers of Other Languages*—because that is the one most commonly used to describe K – 12 school classes and programs for English language learners. It is more favored than *ESL—English as a Second Language*—because students in these programs may already speak a second language. They may be adding English as a third or fourth language.

I also chose to use the term *English language learners* instead of the much more widespread one, *LEP —limited English proficient.* To me, LEP has a decidedly negative connotation. English language learners are not limited; they are learning, and by learning another language they are enriching themselves. Their goal is proficiency in an additional language, and I can see nothing limited about that!

I believe that you will find this text interesting and helpful, and I hope it will encourage you to incorporate many of the strategies and techniques into your regular teaching routines.

I know your efforts will enhance the instructional quality for the ESOL students in your classroom and provide increased opportunities for their academic success.

# PART ONE

# THE CHALLENGE

# CHAPTER I

# TEACHING IN MULTILINGUAL CLASSROOMS: AN INTRODUCTION

## A NEW CHALLENGE

Mr. Elkind teaches social studies in middle school. In every one of his daily classes he has some students who are in the process of learning English. He and the other teachers have often talked about the number of English language learners in their classes. It seems to all of them that each year the number grows.

Mr. Elkind and his colleagues are teachers who really care about what their students are learning. They've talked about their firm belief that these English language learners are intelligent and willing students. At the same time, they also recognize the real need to facilitate their learning experiences and get them more involved in the classroom.

Mr. Elkind, in particular, is concerned because social studies knowledge depends so heavily on reading and research skills. The English language learners in his classes rarely participate in class discussions and activities. He tries to call on them only for what he thinks are the "easy" questions:

*Who won the Civil War—the North or the South? Shin?*
*Luis, can you tell us what year the war ended?*
*Asma, what was the name of the period that followed the end of the Civil War?*

Shihan, Luis, and Asma, upon hearing their names, look uncomfortable. Mr. Elkind's questions are almost always met with silence and downcast eyes. Nothing he's tried has worked very well, and he is becoming increasingly concerned. Helping these students learn has become an important issue to him.

He thinks back to his first years of teaching and remembers many of the challenges he faced, but doesn't recall this as one of them.

Mr. Elkind's memory is accurate. Minority populations all across the United States are growing at an increasing rate. Every state in the nation has experienced this growth, and schools, even in small towns, are facing the challenge of developing programs to help these students learn the English language.

## Learning English: Programs and Goals

The clear objective of every school program for non-native speakers is teaching them to understand, speak, read, and write English. However, the format of instruction varies. Some schools have specialized instruction for their English language learners. In **pull-out** programs, students are sent to classes with special teachers for instruction in English, reading and language arts. In **push-in** programs, the English teacher comes to the language learners' class and teaches them as a group within their own classroom. In other schools, it is the regular English or language arts teacher who is responsible for meeting the special instructional needs of these students.

The simple fact is that all of these approaches deal with only the small part of the school day when these non-native speakers are learning English. For the rest of the day, these English language learners are in regular classes for social studies, math and science, as well as other subjects. Instruction in those areas falls squarely in the domain of the regular classroom teacher —YOU! And if you've already found yourself in this situation, you have probably thought that these students have not developed enough English language skills to understand and participate in the content being delivered in your classroom.

In a sense, this is true. If you teach English language learners in the same manner as you teach the fluent English speakers in your classroom, you are right: the English language learners will not understand or participate. There are, however, quite a number of classroom-tested and proven ways to make what you teach more readily understood.

## In Contrast: The Focus of Content Learning

The shift in student population has brought with it the need for a change in perspective for content classrooms. The traditional focus of teaching or learning to teach social studies, math or science is on the *content* of the subject and on effective approaches and activities to develop specific content competencies in your students.

Compare the content teacher's focus with that of the language arts or English teacher, whose subject matter is the *English language* itself. In these classrooms, the content focuses on the continued development of the skills of language—reading, writing, speaking, and listening. In social studies, math or science classrooms, language is simply the *medium* of instruction. Little if any attention is paid to language because it exists only as the means to deliver the content itself. Now, to help English language learners in their social studies, math and science classes, content teachers must look closely at the medium as well as the content of instruction.

There are many strategies that teachers can bring to their content classrooms to facilitate the comprehension of their subject for their students who are English language learners. With variety, however, comes the need for thoughtful selection. It's not a "one-size-fits-all" plan. Finding what works in your classroom is the challenge presented to you.

## FINDING SOLUTIONS THAT WORK

### Past Attempts

Teachers have, in past times, used several approaches to deal with students who, because of lack of well-developed English language skills, didn't understand the instruction and the content. Unfortunately, these approaches were generally inadequate and ineffective. Perhaps the most common one was simply to ignore these students. After all, how could they be expected to learn content when they didn't even know English!

Other teachers, instead of ignoring the students themselves, simply ignored the fact that these students' needs were different. The students were required to do the same work as the rest of the class, which invariably resulted in the students receiving a poor or failing grade. This was, again, not a particularly adaptive solution.

A somewhat more caring approach was to offer these students "busy work" to fill the class period. Students were kept occupied with classroom housekeeping chores or by coloring pictures, a less stressful but hardly productive approach.

Low expectations and lack of understanding underlay all of these practices. The common belief was that students needed to wait until they learned English well before they could begin to learn content. However, the experiences of creative teachers using innovative approaches clearly demonstrate that this does not have to be the case.

**A Better Way**

Today's teachers, facing ever-increasing numbers of English language learners in their classrooms, are now using solutions that work. More effective approaches involving modifications in curriculum, in teaching, in content, in assignments, and in assessment have been developed so that English language learners can be learning content *while* they are learning English. These approaches are widely referred to as **ESOL strategies.**

ESOL is the acronym that is used for the term *English for Speakers of Other Languages.* It is one of several terms used to refer to programs for English language learners (See Glossary of Acronyms for commonly used terms). ESOL *strategies* are the techniques that are used to modify classroom practices to make content more comprehensible for the ESOL students.

Did you find yourself thinking that this might take a bit of work? Well, the truth is you're right. ESOL strategies *do* take some time to learn, select, plan and implement, but the results are worth it.

## THE REWARDS OF USING ESOL STRATEGIES

Why should teachers expend the effort of developing and using ESOL strategies? The answer to this is simple – because the rewards make it worth your time. These rewards are twofold: both your students and you, the teacher, share in the rewards.

## Rewards to the Students

Using ESOL strategies to deliver content instruction results in a noticeable increase in the level of English language learners' interest and motivation in your classroom. It is not difficult to see why this occurs.

Students most often do not show an interest in something they don't understand. Why would they? Learners basically "turn off" when little or no comprehension is taking place.

And what is one of the most powerful motivators to learning? Interest! Learning is easier, quicker, and more readily retained when it is motivated by interest. We simply pay more attention and learn faster when we are interested in something than when we're not. So, raising the students' level of comprehension promotes interest and motivation.

Using ESOL strategies also helps students develop feelings of self-confidence. There's a wonderful saying: *Nothing succeeds like success.* As English language learners begin to understand the content of instruction, they begin to get an "I can do this" feeling. They begin to develop confidence in themselves as learners. The more they believe they can learn, the better learners they actually become. They grow as learners, both in content knowledge and in English language ability.

A final reward for students involves their cultural and social adjustment. Students moving to the United States from other countries have often come from a successful academic environment, one in which school has been a source of satisfaction and pleasure. Their grades were high and friendships abundant. Now, these same students find themselves in a school environment that is full of frustration and isolation. The teacher who facilitates comprehension for these students by using ESOL strategies is helping to reestablish school as a place of enjoyment. It is an important contribution to these students' adjustment to life in a new country.

## Rewards to the Teacher

*Satisfaction* and *pride* are the words that come to mind here. It's rewarding knowing that you've connected with these students and have engaged them in the learning process. You view your classroom with renewed enthusiasm as you see real learning taking place. You've discovered keys that unlock new pathways to knowledge. Dramatic? Yes, but true. You can actually see that you've made a real difference in the lives of these students.

Your feelings of competence grow. You consider yourself an accomplished professional. That's about as good as it gets as a reward for teaching, don't you think?

# CHAPTER 2
# LANGUAGE, LEARNING, AND CONTENT
# INSTRUCTION

Have you ever thought about what you know when you know a language? You know vocabulary and grammar. You know how to put words together so that someone will understand what you want to say. You know how to choose the right words and phrases to fit a wide variety of circumstances and people. You understand meaning based on intonation (*Really?* means something very different from *Really!*). You know how to read and write, speak, and listen. You, as a fluent speaker of English, possess an enormous amount of language knowledge.

You are probably unaware of all you know. That's because you learned English as your first or native language. Your oral English language skill development began in infancy. You acquired vocabulary and grammar in a seemingly effortless manner.

Because of the naturalness and ease of normal first language development, you've probably not given your own language much thought. Your expertise, as a teacher of social studies, math, or science, lies in your knowledge of the content you teach. Since it is likely that you are less knowledgeable about language and language learning, there are some basic concepts about language that are important to understand in order to help the ESOL students in your classroom.

# LANGUAGE AS A SOCIAL SKILL

Language is a social construct: the purpose of language is communication. Adult speakers of other languages who move to the United States learn some English first to satisfy their basic needs. They often attend English language classes that teach "survival skills," such as asking questions and reading the newspaper want ads so that they can rent an apartment, find a job, and register their children in school.

Children's basic needs are less complex. Children need to make friends with other children. They need to communicate while they play together. They need to participate in the youth culture of athletics, music, TV, video games, movies, fads, and fashion. Children whose native language is not English develop the language skills for these activities by becoming immersed in an English language-rich environment—school. There, for about six hours a day, they receive constant language input through which they learn the language needed to satisfy these needs. It is a process of natural acquisition rather than any type of formal instruction. It bears many similarities to the process of first language development in young children.

The skills these English language learners are developing are called **Basic Interpersonal Communicative Skills** or **BICS,** for short. BICS are the social skills of language, the ones we use to communicate with others in a social environment. It is the language of everyday activities. Children learn BICS with an apparent ease that often awes adult learners. In fact, in children, competent BICS takes only from six months to three years to acquire.

# LANGUAGE AS AN ACADEMIC SKILL

Schools have traditionally judged ESOL students' level of English proficiency based on their conversational skills. But students who function at a high level in face-to-face social interaction may still lack the language skills necessary for learning academic content.

The language that children need to succeed in school is quite different. It is the academic language we use in the classroom.

You're undoubtedly thinking at this point, "That's strange! I'm quite sure I speak the same English in my classroom as I do outside of it, don't I?" The answer to that is both *yes* and *no.*

You *do* use largely the same words, but what teachers ask students to do with language inside the classroom is quite different from what students do with language outside in the real world. So, what do teachers ask students to do?

In an effective classroom, students are asked to engage in thinking skills that involve problem solving and critical thinking. The expression of these skills can takes a number of forms.

Students are often asked to participate in small group or whole class **oral discussions** about issues and ideas. Even more frequently, students are called upon to give oral responses to a teacher's questions.

Students use **listening skills** in increasingly complex ways as they get into the higher grades. Younger children learn content from teachers' spoken words. Older children also need to develop the skill of simultaneous listening, learning, and note taking.

Students use **observation skills** as a tool of learning. Watching science experiments, interpreting graphs, and reading maps, for example, require thoughts to be transferred to language in a special way.

Students are required to use effective *reading skills* in all the content areas. They must read textbooks and other materials to gather information and build knowledge.

Students must often express their thoughts and ideas using *writing skills*. Homework, projects, reports, and research in all subjects almost always take a written form. High-level writing skills are needed to successfully complete them.

These language skills, so commonly required in the classroom, are quite different from those used in social contexts. Social language, or BICS, involves such abilities as recounting anecdotal information and engaging in conversation. The language of the classroom is far more abstract and complex. It makes conceptual demands on language that are not required in BICS.

In the classroom, students are asked, for example, to compare and contrast, explain and justify, or classify and list; and they are required to do these in all the modalities of language—speaking, listening, reading, and writing. These classroom language skills are known as **cognitive academic language proficiency**, or **CALP**.

### Understanding CALP

Another major difference between BICS and CALP lies in the degree of available contextual support for oral or written language. Cummins[1], who contributed the concept of the two types of language proficiency,

---

[1] Cummins, J. (1984). *Bilingualism and Special Education: Issues in Assessment and Pedagogy.* San Francisco, CA: College-Hill Press.

BICS, and CALP, also conceptualized a graphic way to understand language demands (Figure 2.1).

In Cummins's framework for evaluating the difficulty of the language demand in a content activity, the horizontal continuum represents the degree of academic or cognitive challenge in oral and written tasks. The two quadrants on the left side of the chart include oral or written tasks that are either largely social or simply easy. The quadrants on the right represent oral or written tasks that demand higher level reasoning and language skills.

The vertical continuum represents the degree of contextual support. The two quadrants across the

| I<br>Cognitively<br>Undemanding<br>+<br>Context-<br>Embedded | III<br>Cognitively<br>Demanding<br>+<br>Context-<br>Embedded |
| --- | --- |
| II<br>Cognitively<br>Undemanding<br>+<br>Context-<br>Reduced | IV<br>Cognitively<br>Demanding<br>+<br>Context-<br>Reduced |

**FIGURE 2.1Cummins's Framework for Classifying Language and Content Activities** (Modified Format)

top of the chart include highly embedded, contextually supported tasks, while the tasks in the lower quadrants are context reduced.

Oral language becomes contextually supported through facial expressions, gestures, demonstrations, and visual cues from the physical environment. Contextual support for written language includes visual or graphic aids to comprehension of the printed word. Pictures, graphs, charts, tables, and many textbook aids illustrate possibilities for written contextual support.

The quadrants move in difficulty from I to IV. Students will view tasks that are cognitively undemanding and rich in context as easy (Quadrant I). Tasks that are cognitively demanding and severely context reduced (Quadrant IV) will be viewed by students as the hard ones.

Let's look at some specific examples from each of the quadrants. Can you figure out why each activity is assigned to its quadrant?

*Quadrant I*
❑ Engaging in social conversation with peers
❑ Ordering dinner from a picture menu in a fast food restaurant
❑ Listening to a presentation about pet animals that includes pictures and video
❑ Participating in physical education classes

*Quadrant II*
❑ Getting information via the telephone
❑ Ordering dinner from a menu in a formal restaurant

- ❑ Listening to a tape-recorded presentation about caring for pets
- ❑ Reading a list of required school supplies

*Quadrant III*
- ❑ Solving simple math computation problems
- ❑ Solving math word problems using manipulatives and/or pictures
- ❑ Doing a science experiment by following a demonstrations
- ❑ Understanding written text through pictures, graphics, and small group discussion

*Quadrant IV*
- ❑ Solving math word problems without manipulatives or pictures
- ❑ Doing a science experiment by reading directions from a text book
- ❑ Writing  research reports on assigned topics in social studies
- ❑ Listening to a lecture on an unfamiliar topic

Academic tasks that are regularly assigned as classwork and homework are typically cognitively demanding and context reduced (Quadrant IV). For students to experience success with this type of schoolwork, they must have, at the very minimum, grade appropriate cognitive academic language proficiency. ESOL students aren't there yet. Even though they may have good academic language skills in their native language, they're still in the process of developing this proficiency in English. CALP concepts form an important part of the knowledge base that content teachers need in order to select, plan, and use appropriate ESOL strategies in their classrooms.

# LANGUAGE AND CONTENT TEACHING

Academic language skills are complex, cognitively demanding, and situation-specific. They take from five to seven years to reach full development because they are not learned in the same manner as BICS.

CALP is specific to the academic world, and is usually only learned in the classroom. For English language learners to be successful in school, teachers must actively *teach* them this academic language, because this is what their native speaking peers are learning while they are learning the content in their social studies, math and science classes. The process through which native speaking children achieve this ability is a long and complicated one. It is one of the most basic underlying objectives of elementary school curricula.

## How CALP Develops

The elementary school years can be viewed as a six-year course in developing academic thinking and academic language skills. In the primary grades, students learn the basic skills of language. Along with early reading and writing skills, they also begin to learn how to listen, how to observe, and how to think academically. Content learning in the primary grades is taught largely through visual, manipulative, and experiential means. Instruction is facilitated for all students.

English language learners and native speakers alike are going through the same process of learning: they all enter kindergarten needing to learn the most basic skills of language. Because second language learners in the primary grades are so well immersed in an English language environment, they acquire the oral skills of language in a seemingly effortless manner. But there is no doubt that learning the skills involved in reading and writing is an arduous one for all students, regardless of their language background. The primary grades of elementary school focus large blocks of the school day on developing these skills in all students, regardless of their language background.

The intermediate grades of elementary school involve students in language instruction that promotes higher levels of conceptual development and communicative ability. There is a shift in focus from learning to read to reading to learn. Students are now regularly required to think, talk, read, and write about content. They engage in literary criticism (book reports), observations and write-ups of science experiments, research and reports on geography, economy, and culture in social studies, and reading and solving word problems in math.

These experiences in the elementary school years constitute the foundation of academic language learning. Students will be expected to build upon this foundation in the middle and high school years as they use this language knowledge to demonstrate the attainment of specific content knowledge each year in their classes.

English language learners in the primary grades learn content because instruction is context embedded for all students. For English language learners in grades three through twelve, learning content depends on teachers using special ESOL strategies. The strategies available to content teachers to help English language learners progress in the development of content knowledge will be the focus of the rest of this book.

# PART TWO

# THE STRATEGIES

# CHAPTER 3

## STRATEGIES TO MODIFY THE CONTENT OF INSTRUCTION

Effective teachers are adaptive teachers—teachers who understand the importance of modifying curriculum to meet the needs of their students. Within the classroom, skilled teachers adapt, adjust, enrich, and sometimes simplify the content presented in district or state curriculum guides.

For ESOL students, modifying curriculum starts with selecting content to teach.

Selection of content is the foundation upon which all other ESOL strategies will be built. It is the planning decision that structures all other adaptations, and thus, the reason to examine it first.

Content selection begins with a very basic question: *what content do I really want my ESOL students to learn?* The answer to this cannot be *"all of it,"* because if they really could learn all of it they wouldn't be classified as ESOL!

## LANGUAGE DEMAND IN THE THREE CONTENT AREAS

The task of selecting content for English language learners is not quite the same for teachers of the three content areas, social studies, math, and science. Although content choices must be made in all three subjects, the process is considerably easier for science and math teachers than for teachers of social studies for several reasons.

## Language Demand in Math and Science

Science and math concepts more readily lend themselves to extensive visualization. In science, teachers often present concepts through demonstrations, experiments, and graphic representations. In math, teachers generally accompany their oral explanations by writing numerals and symbols on the board and by demonstrating operations with manipulatives. These approaches to teaching decrease the language demand and facilitate the transfer of knowledge and skills learned in the students' first language to those needed in the English language classroom.

Math has another reason for being somewhat easier for ESOL students to comprehend. Students from other countries learn many mathematical concepts at an earlier grade level than their American counterparts. For those students, math is definitely an easier subject because it is largely review.

## Language Demand in Social Studies

Of the major content areas, social studies, presents the greatest challenge for English language learners. It requires high-level literacy skills combined with comprehension of highly abstract concepts. Topics in social studies regularly rely on reading grade-level texts for information, and assignments such as summaries and research reports generally require high-level writing skills. Language demand in social studies is high because the concepts are not readily adaptable to visualization.

An additional challenge for ESOL students is that social studies topics taught in American schools are decidedly culturally based. American history, American government, and the geography of the United States constitute curriculum units that recur with increasing complexity at the elementary, middle, and high school levels. Even the teaching of world history is taught from an American perspective *("...and what was happening at home in America when ...").* Students in other countries do not study these topics in school; their social studies content focuses on the history, government and geography of their own country. ESOL students find social studies difficult because they lack background knowledge of the topics studied in our school systems.

Look back now to Figure 2.1, Cummins's Framework for Classifying Language and Content Activities, in Chapter 2. Math, science, and social studies are all unquestionably academic and cognitively challenging. Math and science, however, are traditionally taught in ways that are more context embedded than social studies. Math and science classrooms often use a hands-on approach to promote active learning. They more readily fit into Cummins's Quadrant III because they can be more heavily embedded in visual contexts. Social studies, in contrast, is more likely to fit into Quadrant IV because of its inherently conceptual nature and is therefore somewhat more difficult for ESOL students to understand and learn.

The differences in the difficulty level for ESOL students, however, do not eliminate the need for teachers of all three subjects to make content choices. Although math and science teachers may be able to include more topics than teachers of social studies, selection of content is still critically important for ESOL students' academic success. How should teachers go about the process of selection? What are some guidelines to inform their choices?

## GUIDELINES FOR SELECTING CONTENT

### Select Priority Topics

The first thing to do is to look closely at the unit topics and subtopics in your curriculum. Narrow your selection of content for ESOL students to priority topics and concepts. A priority topic or concept is one that recurs at various grades of schooling. It is a topic or concept upon which others are built. It is a *core* topic or concept that forms the basis for learning more complex information and ideas. Concepts like *magnetism* in science and *freedom* in social studies are good examples. These concepts form the foundation of knowledge upon which the understanding of more advanced topics will depend.

### Select Topics of Interest

Topics and concepts selected for study should be interesting and engaging. In Chapter 1, we saw that students' interest in a topic motivates learning and facilitates comprehension. Students find themselves interested in topics that relate to previous personal experiences or to prior learning. Relating class topics to the interests of the students in your class makes learning meaningful to them, and meaningful information is more easily learned and retained.

The best way to determine the topics that may interest your ESOL students is to become familiar with their past home and school experiences. The more you learn about them, the more effective you will be in selecting the kind of content they will enjoy learning.

**Select Practical Topics**

Practicality is another element to consider. In weighing the choice between two topics that seem equal in most other ways, select the one that allows more thorough application of the ESOL strategies discussed in the chapters that follow. In other words, choose the topic you think will be easier to make comprehensible to English language learners.

**Select Challenging Topics**

Content modification means *adapting* content, not diminishing it. Topics selected for study need to maintain a high level of academic challenge. A watered-down curriculum may convey a negative message that may stigmatize the ESOL students. Neither they nor the other students in the class should view the work as demeaning, childish or lower on an academic scale. Thoughtful selection of content that is cognitively demanding and requires the use of higher level thinking skills will guard against this possibility.

An effective way to adapt rather than diminish is to think of content in terms of its *depth,* rather than its breadth. Encourage the English language learners in your class to become "experts" in a narrow section of content instead of trying to teach them all the pieces of information included in the entire unit. In science, for example, while the class studies the solar system, your ESOL students can research one planet in depth instead of learning about all of them. In social studies, when the class is learning about the Civil War, your ESOL students can concentrate their efforts on the action and significance of one critical battle or one important military leader. Allow the ESOL students to show off their knowledge by "calling on the experts" when their topics arise in discussion.

Inviting your ESOL students to become specialists in one narrow area is actually a pedagogically sound approach to learning. Long term retention of knowledge is dramatically increased when learning is focused on the principle of *learn more about less*. Students who just "learn facts for the test" often retain the information only until the test is over. Simply stated, we remember interesting information that we studied in depth but quickly forget the memorized bits and pieces.

Think back to your school days. You probably can recall a good deal of information from a major research project you did – perhaps your senior thesis. Years later, you still remember because you really *learned* it in depth.

Another reason you remember this "old" information so well may be because you selected your own topic for the project. If you did, you selected something within the field that interested you. This, too, can be applied to the students in your classroom.

Teachers, through careful guidance and suggestion, can encourage ESOL students to focus on a topic of their own choice for deeper study. Letting their interests determine their selection promotes active involvement in learning.


## YOUR STUDENTS, YOUR CHOICES

Selecting topics and concepts begins the process of curriculum adaptation. The ones you've chosen are important, foundational, cognitively challenging, interesting, and practical.

Take a few minutes now to think about a unit that you teach in one of your classes. Which topics are

28

the ones you want your ESOL students to learn? Your instincts tell you that *everything* you teach is important, and of course, that's true. But the English language learners in your class aren't going to be able to learn all of it. Without using strategies to select content, it wouldn't be surprising to discover that they learned almost none of it. Isn't it much better, then, to choose some of it that they can learn well?

# CHAPTER 4

## STRATEGIES TO MODIFY THE LANGUAGE OF ORAL INSTRUCTION

Have you ever visited a foreign country and tried to understand someone who is speaking to you in their native language? Perhaps it's a language you studied in school, or one that you learned from tapes in preparation for "the big trip."

You did a great job in stopping someone to ask, "Où est la gare?" or "¿Dónde está la playa?" And then you got the answer...but it was not at all easy to understand.

Your first reaction was undoubtedly that the speakers of that language sure speak fast! And it's true: to non-native speakers, native speakers do seem to be speaking fast. That's because the non-native listeners are working on translating what they are hearing into something meaningful and comprehensible. Think of it as *language processing*.

Now let's add a further complication to this little scenario—what you're listening to in the foreign language is not just something social like the price of a souvenir or the directions to the restroom, but instead, a complex academic concept in a science or math or social studies classroom. Quite a challenge, don't you agree?

Oral language, in general, is difficult for language learners because of its ephemeral nature. Words that are spoken simply evaporate into thin air. There is no way to go back over them for review.

Concentrating on the meaning of one spoken sentence means not being able to listen to the next one. Even native speakers have occasional difficulty processing oral language. Imagine, then, what a task it is for ESOL students.

The language of oral instruction, in particular, is difficult for language learners because it is the *medium* through which academic content is delivered. The way oral language is used for lessons involves both *how* the teacher speaks and *what* the teacher says. For English language learners, the *how* is as important as the *what*.

There are quite a large number of strategies for modifying speech. Some involve ways to enhance the clarity of spoken language while others are designed to reduce the complexity of oral instruction. The goal of all speech modifications is to provide language-sensitive instruction so that English language learners who have the social language skills—Basic Interpersonal Communicative Skills, or BICS—can begin to develop the academic language skills, CALP.

## CHANGE THE PACE OF YOUR SPEECH

### Slow Down

The simplest strategy to modify your speech is to slow it down. Speak at a slightly slower pace, but not so slowly that it feels unnatural. *Pause* at natural breaks between phrases or sentences for an extra second or two. Pausing gives ESOL students valuable extra time for language processing.

### Enunciate

Another small modification to speech is to enunciate as clearly as possible. One way to achieve this is to *enhance your intonation* as you speak. Highlight important words by raising or lowering your voice level and your pitch. Giving special intonation to key words in speaking is very similar to underlining, bolding, or italicizing words in writing. Clearly enunciated, well-paced speech with interesting patterns of tonal variation is much more enjoyable to listen to and easier to understand than speech that is rapid and monotonal.

Let's return again to Mr. Elkind, the middle school social studies teacher. On the first day of class, he likes to give his eighth grade students an overview of what they'll be learning in the course of the year. His introduction begins like this:

> "This year we'll be studying the significant historical events that led to the development of our nation's traditions. We'll survey American history with a special emphasis on the nineteenth century. We'll first examine in detail the Declaration of Independence and the Constitution because they're fundamental to the history of the United States. Then we'll study topics such as slavery, the Civil War, Reconstruction, Industrialization, and the United States as a world power."

Where would you pause and which words would you emphasize through rising or falling intonation? Try reading this a little bit more slowly than you normally might, and see what a difference enhanced pausing and intonation can make.

## SIMPLIFY YOUR SPEECH

What do we, as native speakers of English, do that makes our language seem complex to English language learners? A lot—and it's all perfectly normal and correct!

As native speakers, we have learned to speak in patterns that are quite casual and informal, especially when compared with the way we write. There are a number of modifications we can make to our patterns of oral speech to make it easier for ESOL students to understand.

### Avoid Contractions

Try to reduce the use of contractions. Fluent English speakers all contract words when speaking. It's one of the normal differences between spoken and written English. But contractions can easily be misunderstood. Try using the full form of the words— *they are, is not* and *should have,* for example, instead of *they're, isn't,* and *should've.* Using uncontracted forms makes the meaning clearer and also helps to slow down the rate of speech.

### Use Fewer Pronouns

Try to repeat names and other nouns more frequently than you might normally. Pronouns involve some extra language processing and can impede comprehension. Even native speakers occasionally become confused when *it* or *they* is used too many times.

### Use Simple Words

Use high frequency words and use them often. Repeat known words instead of using synonyms. Varying vocabulary to make it more interesting may only cause confusion for ESOL students. The terminology of the minus sign in math is a good example. Look at the variety of ways a simple subtraction problem can be stated:

$$\begin{array}{r} 8 \\ \underline{-5} \end{array}$$

>Subtract 5 from 8.
>Take 5 away from 8.
>Take away 5 from 8.
>8 less 5 equals ...?
>8 minus 5 equals ...?
>5 from 8 equals ...?

Consistent terminology allows ESOL students to process the math concept more easily.

### Teach Meanings of Words Used in New Ways

Learn to recognize words that may have different meanings in different contexts. ESOL students may be familiar with the word *strike*, for example, in the context of baseball. They will need to understand its other meanings when used in the contexts of industry, mining, fishing, bowling, weather, and the military. And that's only its meanings as a noun!

Science words with more commonly used contexts are, for example, *energy, matter, mass, force,* and *kingdom*. Examples of math words with multiple meanings include *table, round, root,* and *power*. No one ever said learning English was easy.

### Explain Idioms and Limit Their Use

Idioms and figurative speech occur regularly in oral language. They give what we say color and interest. Unfortunately, they confuse ESOL students because the meaning of the individual words does not add up to the actual meaning of the whole message. A statement like "She put her foot in her mouth" conjures up a graphic image that doesn't in any way reflect the intended meaning.

In the classroom, a teacher who wanted to check if students understood what was just presented might begin the question session with an enthusiastic opener like, "Okay... I'm going to pitch some practice questions. Let's see who can hit a homerun here!" It definitely adds to the interest level, but your ESOL students are quite likely to look around the room for a baseball and bat.

Try to become aware of examples of idioms and figurative speech used in instruction. An in-class discussion of the Civil War would probably include phrases like

a house divided,
fighting under the Confederate flag,
on the home front, and
loss of lives.

It's not possible to avoid using idioms and figurative speech, nor would we want to. They are one of the ways we personalize and flavor our speech. Becoming aware of using them, however, gives you the opportunity to explain them in a simple way.

**Simplify Your Sentence Structure**
A final way to modify your speech is to keep sentences short and simple in structure. In place of complex sentences with embedded clauses, use sentences that maintain the subject-verb-object structure. Look at this rather long and complex sentence:

The Civil War, which took more American lives than any other war in our history, divided the people of the United States, so that in many families, brother fought against brother.

ESOL students' comprehension would be greatly facilitated by giving the same information this way:

> The Civil War divided the people of the United States. In many families, brother fought against brother. More Americans died in the Civil War than in any other war in American history.

## ENHANCE YOUR WORDS

### Use Gestures

Have you ever heard people say that they couldn't talk if their hands were tied behind their backs? Americans, as well as speakers of many other languages, use their hands to make gestures that supplement their words. It's an important way of enhancing speech.

In classroom instruction, ESOL students will become more involved if you make oral language a visual experience. Be sure to make ample use of the gestures and facial expressions that come so naturally. When you tell your students, "There are three important points to remember," hold up three fingers for your students to see.

Point to any pictures or objects in the classroom that illustrate a particular word. Use pantomime to help explain a new or difficult term. All your students will enjoy it!

### Use Visuals and Graphics

Support your words with graphic representation. Use the "chalk-talk" approach – write key vocabulary words and phrases on the board or on an overhead transparency as you speak them. Show pictures, photos, real objects, maps, graphs, tables, or anything else you can think of to help illustrate the meaning of your words. Capitalize on the saying: *One picture is worth a thousand words.*

Adding visual elements to oral speech contextualizes it. Speech that is more embedded in context is much more easily understood. It is an important way of moving oral instruction from Cummins's Quadrant IV to Quadrant III (Figure 2.1 in Chapter 2).

**Use Repetition and Paraphrase**
Emphasize key points and concepts by summarizing them several times during each class period instead of just at the end. Ask your students questions that start like these:

> *So, what did we just cover?*
> *Who remembers the reasons for_____?*
> *Who can explain the process we just saw?*
> *So, why was _____ important?*

All your students will benefit. Those who know the answers get to "look smart," and those who don't know have another opportunity to hear the information.

Turn back, now, to Mr. Elkind's overview of his eighth grade American history curriculum earlier in this chapter. What advice could you give to him to make his words more comprehensible? What strategies should he use to simplify his speech and enhance his words to make them more comprehensible for the ESOL students in his class?

## CHECK FOR COMPREHENSION

Teachers really like to know that their students understood the lesson they presented. Even more importantly, they want to be able to clarify, repeat, explain, and correct any misunderstandings. So they do comprehension checks by asking:

"Does anyone have any questions?"
"Do you all understand?"
"Does anyone need me to repeat anything?"

Teachers ask these questions out of sincere concern. However, the wording of these questions usually prevents any student from responding. The way these questions are phrased unwittingly asks students who don't understand to raise their hands and identify themselves as "the dumb ones." Which students, ESOL or native speaker, would want to call attention to themselves as the *only ones* who didn't get it? Students would rather suffer confusion in silence than put themselves in such a negative light.

In addition, it may be culturally difficult for ESOL students to ask the teacher a question. There are certain cultures that embrace the belief that asking questions is a rudeness that reflects negatively on the teacher's ability to instruct.

So what words can teachers use that will result in a more effective check for student comprehension? Try one of these instead:

"Question time. Who has a question for me?"
"Question time. What questions do you have?

This simple wording shift implies that questions are a normal and natural part of classroom instruction. It suggests that you *expect* that there will be questions, and that there's nothing wrong with asking them.

You can reinforce this attitude when you respond to the first student who asks a question this way:

*"Great question. Thanks for asking that!"*

*The student not only gets the question answered, but also gets rewarded with praise for asking it. You'll see an immediate difference from the response to "Does everyone understand?"*

## GIVE CLEAR DIRECTIONS

Have you ever been in a class where you've been given directions that you don't understand? You sit there with growing anxiety because you really have no idea what to do. You look around—have others already started working? Are you the only one who didn't understand? Anxiety is never a good way to begin an activity or assignment.

Directions for activities must be understood by all the students in your classroom in order for them to complete the work. Here are five simple steps to follow:

1) State what you want the students to do in a simple, step by step manner.

2) Support your words with written directions on an overhead or on the chalkboard. Keep the written directions in view during the whole assignment so students can refer to them as needed.

3) Model the process and the product. Demonstrate step by step what the students are supposed to do. Show what the finished product should look like. Show several possibilities of finished work if there will be variations.

4) Check for comprehension by asking the students to repeat, step by step, what they are expected to do. Start by asking, "So, what is the first thing we're going to do?" (And, of course, remember to gesture by holding up your index finger.) Go through each step of the activity, adding detail or correcting as necessary.

5) Finish up with "Question time. What questions do you have for me?" You'll be quite pleased with how few you get!


## A COMFORTING THOUGHT

You're thinking that this is quite a bit to remember and try to do, aren't you? Indeed it is, but you need not do it all at once.

Your first step is to think about the way you use oral language in your classroom. An interesting and productive way to do this is to audiotape a lesson you teach. Replaying it will allow you to listen closely to your use of language, and to select one or two areas you'd like to work on. Choose the strategies that you think would help and begin to incorporate them into your patterns of oral instruction. When those feel comfortable, try others, one or two at a time.

Each modification you add enhances the clarity of your oral instruction and facilitates learning for your ESOL students—and quite possibly for some of your native speakers as well!

# CHAPTER 5

## STRATEGIES TO MODIFY THE LANGUAGE OF WRITTEN INSTRUCTION

## PART I: TEXTBOOKS

The written language of content instruction is a real challenge for English language learners. Textbooks contain highly abstract and cognitively demanding concepts, and they are written in language appropriate to the grade for which they are intended. Fortunately, textbook readings can be made more comprehensible to ESOL students (and to native English speaking students who do not read at grade level) through the creative application of modification strategies.

## USING YOUR REGULAR TEXTBOOK

Teachers have varying degrees of control over which textbooks they use in their classes. In many school districts, teachers must simply use the ones they are given, but this is not a problem because many of today's textbooks are written in ways that make them interesting and engaging for students. Students who are English language learners, however, may view them with apprehension because their English reading skills have not yet progressed to the point of being able to bring meaning to the words on these pages.

Reading content textbooks is a frustrating experience for ESOL students. The amount of information often appears overwhelming. Time and effort spent trying to make it understandable generally bring few rewards and little satisfaction. What can you do to make your class textbook more comprehensible for these students?

### Use Textbook Aids

Textbook aids are designed to help organize students' thinking, and well-written textbooks offer them in balanced combinations. Students who understand how to use them have an immediate advantage.

*Chapter titles, section headings*, and *subsection headings* give clues that may help students organize their thinking about the type of information that follows. *Questions and outlines* at the beginning of each chapter focus students' thoughts on the concepts and ideas about to be presented. Chapter *summaries,* topics *for review,* and *questions for reflection or discussion* at the end of chapters allow students to do comprehension checks and engage in critical thinking.

*Glossaries* are also a valuable bonus feature for English language learners. Students should be aware that words that are highlighted in boldface or italic type in the body of the text are defined and explained as a footnote, at the end of the chapter, or in an appendix at the end of the book. In conjunction with the glossary, ESOL students should be encouraged to make liberal use of *bilingual dictionaries* for additional clarification.

*Text boxes* and other *highlighted areas* of key points or section reviews are also valuable, user-friendly features. Some textbooks call attention to information or concepts of particular significance by using boldface or brightly colored type. Finally, some textbooks contain useful and interesting margin notes.

No text is very likely to contain all of these aids to comprehension, but all textbooks contain some. A short lesson on using the ones that appear in your textbook would allow your ESOL students to use them to their advantage.

### Preselect and Preteach Vocabulary

A good way to facilitate comprehension of the textbook is give ESOL students the additional support of knowing the meaning of difficult or technical vocabulary and key concepts before they're assigned to read the chapter. Teachers can preview upcoming chapters, preselect items, and preteach them by working with the ESOL students as a group while the other students are engaged in an independent activity or assignment.

Teach the difficult words and concepts through the use of any of the enhancement strategies presented in Chapter 4. Attempt to discover and point out *cognates,* words that are similar in English and your students' native languages—*democracy* and the Spanish *democracia,* for example. Remember to look for and teach words with multiple meanings.

Encourage students to build their own personal dictionaries, organized in sections of general words and domain-specific or technical words. Promote the generous use of bilingual dictionaries, native language dictionaries, and even translations by a bilingual classmate.

## Highlight Important Concepts

English language learners will find the text easier to read and learn if they can mentally organize the important ideas and concepts presented in the chapter. An effective way to do this is to offer extra credit to native speaking students who are willing to make and share an *outline* or *T-notes* of the chapter.

T-notes are nothing more than a simplified form of an outline. They are formatted in two columns, one to represent main idea and the other to show supporting details and examples (Figure 5.1). Students as early as third grade can begin to learn to use them. They are an excellent way to begin to develop note-taking skills for all students.

| Main Ideas | Details/Examples |
|---|---|
| 1. _____ | 1. _____<br>2. _____<br>3. _____ |
| 2. _____ | 1. _____<br>2. _____<br>3. _____ |
| 3. _____ | 1. _____<br>2. _____<br>3. _____ |

**FIGURE 5.1 Format of T-Notes**

T-notes and outlines serve as a reference and an aid to learning both during the reading process and later as a review. It serves as a powerful strategy that helps to streamline the reading process. It may even become a useful tool for some of your native speaking students.

## Group ESOL Students to Discuss the Text

Reading, especially reading assigned as homework, has traditionally been viewed as an individual activity. Students are supposed to read at home and arrive in class the next day prepared for discussion. ESOL students will be able to learn more during these discussions by meeting together in small groups first to discuss the readings from the text.

It is a good idea to structure these small group meetings by preparing several questions about key concepts in the assigned reading that will serve to organize the discussion. The give and take of discussion, even in the students' native language, affords English language learners the opportunity to negotiate their knowledge and increase their understanding of information in the printed text.

## Audiotape the Text

It should not come as a surprise that reading comprehension and retention rise when readers simultaneously see and hear information.[2] As a matter of fact, one way that a good reader attempts to comprehend a difficult text is to read the passage out loud. Hearing the printed words assists in producing meaning.

---

[2] Closed captioning TV and video has been shown to be an effective aid to comprehension for both native and non-native learners. Closed captioning was originally developed for the hearing impaired. It uses subtitles that put into print the exact words that are being spoken on the screen. Most monitors and televisions are prewired to receive closed captioning programming.

ESOL students benefit from seeing and hearing text in other ways as well. They learn pronunciation of unfamiliar words. They may make new associations of words in their oral and written forms, words that they may know in spoken form but not recognize in writing because they are spelled quite differently than they are pronounced. And a final advantage concerns *homophones,* words that are pronounced the same but are spelled differently and have different meanings— *there-their-they're,* for example. Simultaneously seeing and hearing these words in context may help students to understand and remember the different meanings and usages.

Again for extra credit, a student in your class can read entire chapters or important sections of the textbook into a tape recorder. (The student is actually reinforcing understanding and enhancing learning by doing this.) ESOL students can listen to the tape at home while reading the text. Using this multimedia approach facilitates comprehension.

**Use Learning Logs**

Learning logs are basically structured journals based on reading assignments from the textbook. Students use them while they are attempting to read the assigned pages.

The format of the learning log is quite simple (Figure 5.2). With minor adaptations, it can also be used for a wide range of activities beyond text readings. For example, in a science class, the first column could be changed for use with experiments or demonstrations, or in a math class, for use in oral presentations of new concepts. In any content class, it can be used when videos or filmstrips are used to present new information. The uses of learning logs are limited only by the imagination and creativity of the teacher.

It is important to set aside time during the school day to address the issues, questions, or difficulties that the students have noted in their logs. To save teachers' time, instead of meeting with individuals or small groups, students themselves can meet to discuss their entries. They can help each other by exchanging understandings, answering each other's questions, and clarifying vocabulary. Encourage their independence, but offer your support as needed. Students should note in their logs the new understandings that result from these discussions.

| Text Pages | What I Understood | New or Difficult Vocabulary | Questions I Want to Know |
|---|---|---|---|
|  |  |  |  |

**FIGURE 5.2 Format of a Learning Log**

Learning logs give ESOL students another way to become engaged in the process of negotiating knowledge and increasing their understanding of the text. Learning logs also form an excellent set of notes for ongoing or summary review of the material.

**Two "Extra" Strategies**

The last two suggestions in this section should be used with discretion. They are included here because the more strategies teachers know, the better they will be prepared to meet the needs of all their students. Teachers may find themselves in situations where one of these strategies may seem appropriate.

The first of these less-than-ideal strategies is to pair a bilingual student of the same language background with the English language learner to translate concepts and information from the readings. The problem with this approach is that it places a heavy burden on the translator, and may lead to the language learner's dependence on the translation and the translator.

The second strategy is to obtain an alternate textbook for the English language learners in your class. You might consider using a text that is written at a lower reading level, or one written in the students' native language. This strategy, too, presents several problems.

Using an alternative textbook is stigmatizing, especially one written at a lower level. It conveys the attitude that those who use it are less capable than the others in the class.

Using a native language textbook, assuming one is even available, also has several drawbacks. The most serious of these is that it will promote reliance on the native language text at the expense of the English language one. Much like using a translator, it may slow down the development of English language skills.

An additional difficulty with attempting to find native language texts arises if your ESOL students are from several language backgrounds. How can you expect to find books on the topics in each of the languages spoken by the students in your classroom? And if you can't find native language textbooks for all, is it fair to find texts for only some?

You may be thinking, at this point, about what type of situation might even start you thinking about using these strategies. When might they be appropriate?

If you receive a student in your content class who is a true English language beginner, these last two strategies are a better choice than doing nothing. They are probably the best you can do for a while because, at the very least, they allow the student to learn some content and they show that you care.

## CHOOSING A TEXTBOOK

Teachers who are given the opportunity to select textbooks for their classes are the lucky few. They are in a most fortunate position when they know what to look for and how to make the choice.

Textbooks are an expensive item on a school or district budget, and they are generally purchased on a rotating basis, by grade and content area. New ones must often be chosen from a list of state adopted books. Nonetheless, when selection time comes, teachers need a set of guidelines to help them make a good decision.

The guidelines focus exclusively on the main textbook that the students will use. Peripherals like workbooks, videos, teacher's guides, and the like are valuable but can't make up for a difficult or poorly designed textbook. Following the guidelines suggested here will result in having textbooks in your classroom that maximize the potential for ESOL students' academic success. However, these guidelines really have a much wider application. All students, of all subjects, and in all grades, will enjoy textbooks that exhibit the very same characteristics and qualities that are so helpful to English language learners.

**First Impressions**

What is your very first thought when look at a new textbook? What is your immediate reaction as you first open it up and fan through the pages? These are the questions that should begin your examination of the textbook.

First impressions often shape our long-range views. Have you ever had the experience of opening a textbook for a course that you were about to begin and thinking, "Uh oh, this course is going to be really hard!" What you're reacting to is not the difficulty of the course, but the perceived difficulty of its textbook, and that perception is based largely on how the book looks. We really *do* judge a book by its cover! Initial reactions to a textbook can determine your students' attitudes to the whole course.

First impressions generally involve the overall appeal of the book – its style, even its weight and size. Textbooks that "invite" the reader in are those that are attractive. Overall appearance determines whether or not the contents look *learnable*.

**Layout**

The textbook layout determines its overall attractiveness. The list that follows will help you focus on individual items that determine whether the textbook has "student appeal."

- ❑ Length of sections and chapters
    - Information that is broken up into smaller chunks looks more learnable.
- ❑ Size and style of the typeface
    - Slightly larger type and more space between lines of print make text easier to read.
- ❑ Amount of white space on the page
    - Wider margins and more space between sections make content look more comprehensible.
- ❑ Paper quality and color
    - Glossy white paper makes print easier to read than paper that is ivory colored and has a matte finish.
- ❑ Amount and variety of graphic design features
    - An interesting *cover* invites the reader to open the book.
    - *Illustrations* embed context and make the text more comprehensible. Look for charts, maps, graphs, diagrams, and tables that are colorful, interesting, and varied.
    - *Pictures* and *photographs* enhance text. They should be modern looking, appropriate, and culturally diverse.
    - Simple *graphics* emphasize and clarify teaching points and key concepts. Look for abundant use of boxes, bullets, bolding or color.
    - *Balance of graphics to text* should be appropriate. Pages should not appear dense or cluttered.

**Subject Matter**

No matter how appealing its layout, a textbook is good only if it meets the requirements of your curriculum and the needs of your students. Here are some questions to think about as you conduct your review:

- ❑ Is the content suitable and interesting to the age, grade, and academic level of the students?
- ❑ Is the content current and accurate?
- ❑ Is the content a good fit with the curriculum?
- ❑ Are the topics presented in a logical manner?
- ❑ Are new concepts supported with appropriate amounts of background information and review?
- ❑ Are topics covered in appropriate depth?
- ❑ Are topics explained in a simple and clear manner?
- ❑ Is new or technical vocabulary clearly defined when it is introduced?

**Textbook Aids**

Textbook aids are designed to form a system of support to promote students' understanding of the material. Textbooks vary widely in their use of special aids to comprehension, not only in how many they include, but also in type, clarity, and format.

While all students gain from using textbook aids, ESOL students, in particular, profit from them. Examine possible textbooks with these questions in mind:

- ❑ Is the table of contents specific enough to locate categories of information?
- ❑ How inclusive is the index?
- ❑ Is there a glossary? If so, how are the words highlighted in the text? How clear are the definitions and explanations of words listed in the glossary?

- Are there appendices? Do they contain interesting supplementary information?
- Is there an overview or outline at the beginning of each chapter?
- Are there frequent summaries at the ends of subsections and at the end of each chapter?
- Are there questions or topics for review or for critical thinking at the end of each chapter?

Textbook aids for ESOL students also include some of the items listed in the layout section. Charts, maps, photos, pictures, diagrams, graphs, and tables add visual context to print. Words in boldfaced type call attention to key concepts and important words and phrases, while boxes and bullets highlight important information. These are all elements that facilitate comprehension by making the context more heavily embedded.

**Just One Last Question**

The perfect textbook for your class probably doesn't exist, but some certainly come much closer to your ideal than others. When you've narrowed the field down to the final contenders based on these guidelines, the time has come to ask one last question: *Is this a textbook I would like to use?*

# CHAPTER 6

## STRATEGIES TO MODIFY THE LANGUAGE OF WRITTEN INSTRUCTION

## PART II: ASSIGNMENTS

Mr. Elkind, the middle school social studies teacher, enjoys seeing his students actively involved in their own learning. His classroom is a dynamic place, filled with daily activities designed to develop and deepen his students' understanding of the topics they're studying.

For every unit he creates exciting and unusual ideas for projects and encourages his students to choose the ones that interest them—anything from reading historical novels to doing specialized research on the Interne. His homework assignments build background for lessons or reinforce and enrich what was learned in class. Most of the students love his class because he makes history come alive.

Wonderful? Yes, but stop now and think about the language demand of these activities. Mr. Elkind's assignments and projects involve a heavy load of reading, research, and writing. For the English language learners in his class, history is more frustrating than lively.

What assignments can ESOL students do that maintain a high level of cognitive challenge and, at the same time, reduce the language demand? Teachers need to think beyond the traditional written reports and oral presentations so often used in classrooms and find appropriate, engaging alternative means and products. The goal is to build conceptual understanding of content while keeping the language as simple as possible. Strategies that achieve this objective are visual and hands-on in nature.

The strategies presented in this chapter are of two types: first, strategies that suggest ideas to modify the regular assignments you use with the whole class, and then, strategies that offer ideas for alternative but parallel activities.

## MODIFYING WHOLE CLASS ASSIGNMENTS

There are several approaches to reducing language demand to make your regular assignments more appropriate for the English language learners in your classes. These modifications are widely adaptable for use with many types of homework and in-class activities.

### Offer a Word Bank

For assignments that require simple, short answers to a set of questions, consider using a word bank. Word banks are simply lists of word choices. Students select words from the list to correctly answer the questions in an assignment. To encourage thoughtful processing when students get down to the last few word choices, be sure to include several extra words that are related to the topic.

This strategy also works well when students are, for example, labeling parts of a diagram in science or doing map work in social studies. English language learners can focus their attention on content because the language demand has been lowered.

### Assign Fewer Questions

Many assignments require writing longer answers to a set of questions. An assignment that seems reasonable for your native speaking students can easily appear overwhelming to your English language learners. Reduce the number of questions for them by selecting the ones that seem more central to the topic, and simply eliminate the rest.

### Evaluate for Content Only

Evaluate the work of ESOL students for accuracy of content only. While you probably require the use of full sentences, correctly written, as a normal part of your regular assignments, try to remember that if your English language learners were able to do that, they wouldn't be classified as ESOL. So, for them, read their assignments solely for content information. Accept grammar and spelling errors as long as the content is correct. Accept single word or short phrase answers instead of full sentences. Think about the *message* they're sending, not about the *means* through which it is sent.

### Offer Models and Outlines

When assignments involve paragraph writing, consider giving the ESOL students a model, an outline, or a pre-formatted sheet to follow. In science classes, for example, students are often assigned to write reports describing experiments, demonstrations, or activities done in class. Giving English language learners a model or pre-formatted form (Figure 6.1) to follow allows them to concentrate on the cognitive processing of what they learned in class instead of having to focus on creating language for the report.

```
We wanted to show that _____
_____.

We used (materials) _____ , _____ ,
_____ , _____ , _____.

The first thing we did was _____
_____.

The second thing we did was _____
_____.

The third thing we did was _____
_____.

What happened was _____
_____.

This happened because _____
_____.

This shows that _____
_____.
```

**FIGURE 6.1 Model for Write-up of Science Demonstration**

These modifications in regular assignments can be tremendously helpful for English language learners. Even small changes, like the inclusion of a word bank, can mean the difference between frustration and success. The important thing is to look at assignments from the vantage point of your ESOL students. Anticipating the areas of language difficulty and making appropriate modifications will be surprisingly productive.

## DEVELOPING ALTERNATIVE ASSIGNMENTS

The second type of strategy involves developing parallel assignments for ESOL students. The goal is to create engaging activities that maintain a high level of cognitive challenge but lower the language demand. Here are some interesting ways to accomplish this.

### Diagrams, Maps and Charts

When your regular class assignment involves descriptive writing, let your English language learners complete a diagram, map, or chart instead. In addition to labeling or naming parts, you may want them to add supplementary or related pieces of information in the form of words or short phrases with arrows indicating relationships.

### Sequenced Pictures

ESOL students can show their understanding by drawing or arranging sequenced pictures. While the other students are writing up the results of an in-class science demonstration for homework, your ESOL students can be doing the same assignment using graphics rather than writing. Sequenced pictures can depict several steps or stages, or they can be as simple as "before and after."

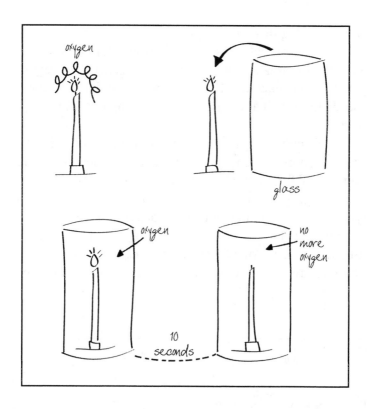

**FIGURE 6.2 Sequenced Pictures**

After the pictures have been drawn or arranged, you may want to have students add some written information. Parts of each picture can be labeled. Or descriptive words or phrases can be written under each one. For students who are real ESOL beginners, you can even include a word bank.

Look at the information conveyed in Figure 6.2. The high beginner ESOL student who did these drawings clearly understood the demonstration, but would have had a difficult time trying to explain it in a written report.

## Graphic Organizers

You probably use graphic organizers (also called advance organizers and visual organizers) as a regular part of your teaching. But did you know that you could use them as valuable alternative assignments for ESOL students?

Graphic organizers are interesting and easy for English language learners to work with. They come in a number of forms, each designed for a specific purpose. The type of graphic organizer you assign depends on the type of information called for in the regular assignment.

The graphic organizer with the widest application uses the concept of *clustering* or *webbing* (Figure 6.3). Students are able to depict complex relationships among

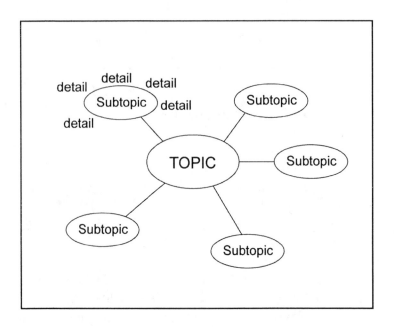

**FIGURE 6.3 The Cluster or Web**

elements with a minimum amount of language. This type of organizer is particularly useful for explaining topics with multiple elements. It would be appropriate to use one in social studies, for example, to show the causes of World War II or factors influencing immigration to the United States in the early 1900s, and in science, to categorize, classify and describe substances and structures.

A more tightly controlled form of clustering is the ***problem-solving organizer*** (Figure 6.4). Its purpose

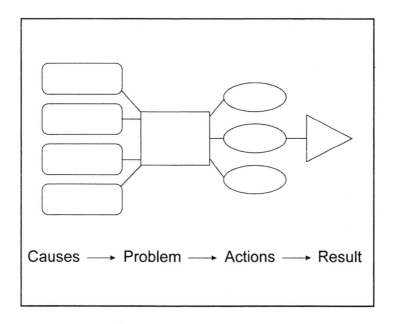

Causes ⟶ Problem ⟶ Actions ⟶ Result

**FIGURE 6.4 The Problem Solving Organizer**

is to show sequential cause and effect. It can be effectively used when more direct relationships and patterns need to be emphasized.

This type of organizer is structured around a central problem or issue. The causes of the problem, actions taken to correct the problem, and results of these actions are shown in graphic form. Select this for your ESOL students as an alternative to a written report, for example, on an environmental issue.

A *Venn diagram* (Figures 6.5 and 6.6) is the graphic of choice when an assignment is of a compare-and-contrast nature. This type of organizer shows similarities and differences among two or three concepts, events, people, or things. Because the language demand is reduced to single words or phrases, English language learners can focus on the content.

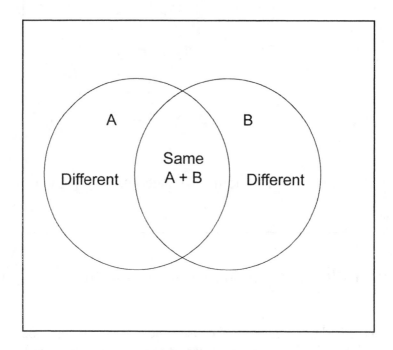

**FIGURE 6.5 Venn Diagram Comparing Two Things**

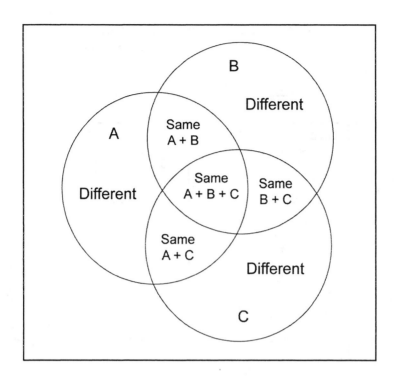

**FIGURE 6.6 Venn Diagram Comparing Three Things**

The *timeline*, as its name implies, shows chronological sequences and temporal relationships. Timelines can be drawn to record developments over periods as short as seconds or as long as thousands of years. They can, for example, illustrate changes in matter over a period of seconds or minutes or depict historical events over one century. Timelines are simple and readily adaptable, a good combination of qualities for ESOL students.

A final graphic organizer to consider is the *matrix* (Figure 6.7). It is designed in the form of a grid, and serves to visually compare key variables across several categories. The matrix is versatile and has wide

| Qualities ——→ Items to Compare ↓ | #1 | #2 | #3 | #4 | #5 |
|---|---|---|---|---|---|
| A | | | | | |
| B | | | | | |
| C | | | | | |
| D | | | | | |
| E | | | | | |

**FIGURE 6.7 The Matrix**

application. Matrix grids can be filled in with a plus or minus sign to denote presence or absence, a number denoting a specific amount or percentage, or a short descriptive word. This type of graphic organizer works well to compare, for example, characteristics or qualities of a set of substances in science (Figure 6.8). In social studies, it could be used to compare the geographic or economic features of several countries or regions.

| MINERALS | | | | | |
|---|---|---|---|---|---|
| Specimen ↓ | Luster | Cleavage | Hardness | Color | Other? |
| A | | | | | |
| B | | | | | |
| C | | | | | |
| D | | | | | |
| E | | | | | |

**FIGURE 6.8 Sample Matrix**

**Hands-on Assignments**

Manipulatives and other hands-on learning materials allow ESOL students to demonstrate their understanding of abstract concepts in a concrete, visual manner. English language learners, especially beginners, may enjoy showing mastery of a concept by creating dioramas or models, or by presenting an interesting experiment, exhibit, or demonstration.

The alternative assignments you choose will depend on the students' level of English fluency. Students need to start with simple tasks and move on to more complex ones. Remember that CALP, or academic language, develops slowly over a long period of time.

Giving ESOL students modified or alternative assignments along with a healthy dose of encouragement offers them a good possibility of achievement. You will see an immediate, positive effect in your classroom when you begin using these strategies. Whether you modify your regular written assignments or create new ones for your English language learners, you will be pleased with the changes you see.

# CHAPTER 7
## STRATEGIES TO MODIFY THE TECHNIQUES OF INSTRUCTION

Students learn because teachers teach – a simple truth. It's also true that students learn more and are more motivated to learn when they have good teachers. It is unlikely than anyone would take issue with the statement that nothing is better than a good teacher is.

What do you need to know to be a good teacher to the English language learners in your classroom? How can you make your classroom instruction more accessible to them? What strategies will facilitate their comprehension and learning?

The answers to these questions may surprise you. Many of the ideas presented in this chapter are teaching techniques that facilitate learning for all students. In fact, you may already be using some of them.

These strategies are included here because for ESOL students they are more than just good teaching techniques – they form the foundation for comprehensible instruction. For English language learners, these are the strategies that open the door of understanding. Incorporating these strategies into your classroom instruction makes the difference that allows the ESOL students in your classroom to learn the content you are teaching.

## THE IMPORTANCE OF BACKGROUND KNOWLEDGE

Activating students' prior knowledge is a strategy that is essential to effective teaching because it is the students' own background knowledge that forms the building blocks upon which new learning is built. Activating background knowledge and experience makes learning meaningful, awakens interest in the topic, and increases motivation. All students, not only ESOL students, benefit from making explicit connections between past and present learning. If this is so, why, then, is this a special issue for English language learners?

School curriculum is planned around the assumption of common academic background and personal experience for students at each grade level. However, students coming from other countries may have very different individual, cultural and academic backgrounds and experiences than those of other students in your class. Teachers must not only activate background for ESOL students, but also determine that they have the *relevant* background to be successful in learning the new content. Because prior knowledge is so fundamental to new learning, teachers must *build* background knowledge where none exists. The strategies presented in this section will simultaneously activate prior knowledge for students who have it and build new knowledge for those who need it.

\*  \*  \*  \*  \*  \*

## STRATEGIES TO ACTIVATE BACKGROUND KNOWLEDGE

### Use Brainstorming

Brainstorming is an effective strategy to introduce a new topic. It activates students' background knowledge and engages their interest, and, at the same time, helps you determine whether or not your students have enough background knowledge to move ahead.

Start by writing the topic word on the chalk board. Accompany it with the open-ended question, *"What comes to mind when I say the word _____?"* As students respond, write their words and phrases around the topic word to form a graphic organizer. Accept all answers, even wrong ones, by responding with something like, "Well, let's save these answers so we can come back to them later to see which are true and which ones are not."

With the display left in place, you also have an excellent means of review. By pointing to a specific word or phrase, students can talk about what they learned in this lesson. They can add new words and phrases, correct misconceptions, and see what is yet to be covered. As a way of activating prior knowledge, this one is particularly easy and advantageous.

### Try "Think-Pair-Share"

Another effective approach to activating prior knowledge and, at the same time, encouraging participation is through a type of activity called Think-Pair-Share. Start with the same open-ended question as in the brainstorming activity, but this time, instead of asking for an immediate response, give students one or two minutes to jot down any related words or phrases they can think of. Then, for the next minute or two, they expand their lists by discussing them with a partner.

Finally, you invite students to share their ideas with the rest of the class. It gets the students actively involved in the topic and guarantees participation.

**Use a K-W-L Chart**

A graphic organizer that complements the Think-Pair-Share activity is the K-W-L chart (Figure 7.1). Students are asked to write what they already *know* (or think they know) about a topic in the K column. They then discuss what they *want* to know with a partner or in a small group to complete the W column. They complete

| What do I know? | What do I want to know? | What have I learned? |
|---|---|---|
|  |  |  |

**FIGURE 7.1  K – W – L Chart**

the L column at the end of the lesson by listing what they *learned*. Students can make daily entries in each of the columns as an ongoing means of activating their prior knowledge and stimulating critical thinking.

**Personalize Your Lesson**

Asking students to contribute their own experiences is a great way to activate prior knowledge and experience. It stimulates interest by inviting personal contributions to begin a unit.

An example may best explain this concept. Before introducing the Civil War, you could talk about the concept that differences among individuals and groups can lead to conflict. Your ESOL students may have first-hand knowledge of conflicts based on political, ethnic, or religious differences in their own countries. Other students may want to share stories about "family feuds." Sharing this type of knowledge is interesting and allows you to draw comparisons and make generalizations.

Students – all students – enjoy sharing personal experiences. It's an exciting way to begin a new topic.

**Make Daily Linkages**

Ongoing lessons also benefit from making daily linkages of new concepts to students' past experience, past knowledge, and past learning. Start daily lessons with openers that activate learning from previous lessons on the same topic or concept. Making explicit connections serves as a form of review and reinforcement. By regularly stimulating background knowledge, you facilitate students' continuing concept development and increase the potential for learning and retention.

\* \* \* \* \* \*

# INCREASING TEACHER-STUDENT
# INTERACTION IN THE CLASSROOM

Students thrive in classrooms where teachers promote learning through participation and interaction. Do you interact with *all* the students in your classroom?

**Monitor Your Interaction Patterns**

An interesting way to systematically monitor your interaction with students is to videotape a class you teach. Watch the taped lesson, noting on a class seating chart precisely who you called on and how many times. You may make some unexpected discoveries.

Many teachers are amazed to find that they have a distinct *action zone*, that is, a localized area of the classroom that they favor by looking at and calling on the students in that section much more than the others.

Other teachers have found that they had neglected to call on several students in the class, even though they felt sure they had involved everyone.

If you liked what you saw, that's great. But if not, you need a system to offer all students the opportunity to participate. Teachers have used a number of techniques, from the quite simple – checking off names on a class list or seating chart – to the creative – writing student names on popsicle sticks that were then placed in a cup and randomly drawn by the teacher. Use what works for you.

**Encourage Participation**

Calling on all the students in your class does not necessarily mean that each will participate. To encourage your ESOL students, start by trying to make friendly eye contact and smiling at each of them. Then consider ways to lower both the language difficulty of your questions and the anxiety of answering them.

Select the *types of questions* you direct to your English language learners. They will have much less difficulty responding to questions requiring short answers. Pattern your questions as yes/no, either/or, or one-word response questions.

*So the South won the Civil War, right?*
*Which one is a mammal – a whale or a shark?*
*Who can give me another example of a mammal?*

Questions such as these are considered lower order because they ask for simple recall of information. You undoubtedly ask your students higher order questions requiring reasoning or inferencing ability as well. You can get your ESOL students involved in this type of question by directing a question like, *"Do you agree with Yaset's answer?"* Follow up with *"Why?"* or *"Why not?"*

Watch your ESOL students' faces when you direct a general question to the whole class. Sometimes you can sense that certain students would like to try to answer but can't quite bring themselves to raise their hands. This would be a good time to invite their participation. Assist them in their efforts by encouraging them to support their words with visual aids by pointing—to pictures, to places on maps, or to words on the blackboard.

Feelings of anxiety hamper students' ability to participate. Anxiety interferes with effective thought processing.

You can *lower anxiety* for your ESOL students by giving them extra *wait-time*, the time you give students to think and respond after you've asked a question. Your usual wait time may not be adequate for the English language learners because along with thinking of the answer, they must also process the language of your question and their response. Wait-time of five seconds for simple questions, and as much as ten to twenty seconds for more complicated questions, helps to lower the feelings of anxiety that often accompany being called on to produce an answer.

Acknowledging incorrect answers with *"Good try," "Almost,"* or *"Thank you for trying"* is another way to lower the anxiety of participation. These responses lessen the stigma of wrong answers and encourage continued attempts at participation.

Giving students a face-saving manner of not answering a question also lowers anxiety levels. It can be accepted practice in your class for students to respond with "Pass" or by the student calling on another student for assistance.

## INCREASING STUDENT-STUDENT INTERACTION IN THE CLASSROOM

### Do More Small Group Work

Group work promotes concept acquisition for all students, but especially for English language learners. Social interaction in pairs or small groups offers a natural setting that encourages the negotiation of meaning in a non-threatening environment. Small groups allow ESOL students more comfortable conditions to explore new vocabulary, to attempt oral communication, and to clarify knowledge through the exchange of culturally familiar examples and comparisons. Many students learn better by negotiating meaning with peers within the safety of small groups.

Student-student interaction also includes pairing students to work together. Partners or buddies enhance each other's understanding, as in the saying *two heads are better than one.* Consider allowing your English language learners to produce a pair product while the other students work individually. Students may be able to accomplish together an assignment that neither one of them could complete alone.

### Try Peer Tutoring

Peer tutoring allows students to learn from each other while the teacher takes the role of the facilitator who monitors the students' understanding and progress. Those who are doing the tutoring are clarifying their understanding by explaining, and those who are being tutored benefit from personalized instruction in a non-threatening setting.

### Big Benefits from Small Groups

You may be like many teachers who, for a variety of reasons, just don't do much group work in class even though you know that group work is good[3]. What you may not know is how *very good* group work really is.

The benefits of group work and peer tutoring are enormous. Small group interaction promotes concept acquisition and cognitive growth. It offers an excellent opportunity for students to use academic language in a meaningful way. It personalizes learning and instruction.

---

[3] For an excellent and delightfully written discussion of how to make your group work successful, read Chapter 12 of *Teaching by Principles: An Interactive Approach to Language Pedagogy (2nd Ed.)* by H. Douglas Brown (Prentice Hall Regents, 2001)

It has the ability to change students' attitudes toward content and to school in general. It ultimately raises students' feelings of self-confidence.

In pair and small group work, one plus one really does add up to more than two. Try it. You will be pleased with the result.

## ENHANCING TEACHING TECHNIQUES

Creative approaches to instructional delivery are important for English language learners. ESOL students need to learn not just by listening, but also by watching and doing. Students learn concepts faster when instructional approaches include visual and hands-on elements.

### Write Your Words

Start by adding a visual dimension to your classroom instruction. Write key words on the board or on an overhead transparency as you say them. Seeing a word in print at the same time as hearing it spoken facilitates comprehension for ESOL students.

### Illustrate Your Words

Incorporate *pictures*, photos, sketches, maps, charts, tables, and graphs. Make ample use of the overhead projector. Copy visuals onto transparencies and refer to them as you talk. Supplement class lectures and discussions with filmstrips, slides, videotapes, and CD-ROM programs. Encourage students to find and share interesting websites on the Internet.

Try to get in the habit of using *graphic organizers* as a regular part of your teaching. Graphic organizers help English language learners see relationships and understand vocabulary and concepts.

Bring in *realia* to interest the students. Realia are authentic, real world objects that illustrate a concept in ways that allow students to make meaningful connections to their own lives. Examples of realia are using bank deposit slips and check registers for a unit on banking and working with copies of actual floor plans to calculate square footage. Ask students to contribute their own realia. It may be an interesting cultural experience for all.

### Demonstrate Your Words

Show your students how to find an answer or solve a problem by *demonstration* and *modeling*. Take your students through the step-by-step process that explains how to reach the end result.

This technique is particularly applicable to solving word problems in math. Demonstrate how to break the problem down into smaller parts by actually sharing the questions you asked yourself and showing the steps you took. You are modeling useful strategies to reach the solution. Accompanying this approach with the use of *hands-on manipulatives* takes word problems from the abstract to the concrete.

### Be Dramatic

Make your lessons not only comprehensive but also memorable by hamming them up! Dramatize, emote, pantomime, stage reenactments— have a good time! It's a sure way to get students to remember material and probably you, too.

\* \* \* \* \* \*

# TEACHING LEARNING STRATEGIES

Learning strategies are the techniques used to make information easier to understand, to remember, and to apply. They are the "tricks" of the learning trade.

Students' school success is related to their skill as learners. More effective learning strategies make students more resourceful and independent. They become more successful students. Teaching learning strategies promotes the concept that all students can be successful. It is a motivating belief for the learner.

## Types of Learning Strategies

Learning strategies fall into three basic categories. The first type, called metacognitive strategies, organize the students' thinking about learning. These are the ones that help plan, monitor, and evaluate learning.

The second type, called cognitive strategies, offer means of manipulating and practicing the material so that it is learned. This category includes such strategies as summarizing, classifying, extending the known to the unknown, making lists, and taking notes.

The third type, called social strategies, involve social interaction and affective approaches to learning. Studying in groups and questioning for clarification are good examples of strategies based on social interaction, and techniques that lower anxiety and self-reward success are examples of affective strategies.

## Learning Strategy Development

How do you teach learning strategies? Whole books have been written to answer this question, but a brief answer will at least start you thinking in the right direction.

Start by looking over the material that you want the students to learn with this question in mind: *How would I go about learning this?* Would you highlight and then summarize key concepts? Would you make a list classifying concepts according to their attributes? Would you memorize a rule and then attempt to apply it to other problems? The number of possible learning strategies is large.

Decide on several good ways to learn the material. Explain to your students your own thought processes and how you would go about learning the information. Follow up by demonstrating and modeling through a step-by-step process. Finally, give your students practice in applying the learning strategy. Encourage them to evaluate and discuss whether and why it worked for them.

By repeating this process, students build a repertoire of learning strategies from which to draw for future reference. Keeping a learning strategy log or journal produces an actual menu-type source of referral.

## AND A FEW FINAL SUGGESTIONS

### Allow Extra Time

Plan to give your English language learners extra time for practice and for application of new concepts. Remember that they are learning English at the same time that they are learning *in* English.

### Be Creative with Homework

Give different assignments to different groups depending on language ability. Modify assignments for homework using the ideas presented in the previous chapter.

Write daily homework assignments on a special section of your chalkboard to avoid the hurried rush of words at the end of the class period. Make sure students know that homework information will be written in the same place every day.

One very creative teacher created a homepage for her classes on the Internet. She posted daily homework assignments there along with other interesting messages and reminders to students and their parents. Students with computers at home looked forward to reading the new postings, and students without home computers were excited to get extra time every day to use the ones in the classroom.

There are several websites[4] that offer this service at no charge to teachers. It's definitely a win-win situation.

Using these strategies to modify your teaching techniques will facilitate the comprehension of content for your English language learners. Your students will move from spectators in your classroom to active participants in the process of their own learning.

---

[4] This particular teacher used www.schoolnotes.com.

# CHAPTER 8
# STRATEGIES TO MODIFY THE TECHNIQUES
# OF ASSESSMENT

Let's return again to Mr. Elkind's middle school social studies class. While Mr. Elkind feels he needs to do more to get his ESOL students involved in learning, the one area that really has him stumped is assessment.

Mr. Elkind's tests are a mixture of multiple-choice questions, which he uses to check on his students' grasp of the basics, and short essay questions that require a higher level of critical thinking. He understands why his ESOL students don't do well on the essays – he knows these questions are heavy in language demand. What puzzles him is why they also don't do well on the multiple-choice sections. It seems to him that these are simple questions that require only that students recognize the right answer.

And grading is a problem, too. Most of his ESOL students earn grades of D or F on his exams, but he hates to write this on their papers. So what grade should he give them? He feels that giving them the grade they actually earned will make them feel like failures – all the low grades will do is lower their self-esteem and motivation even further. And he thinks that it's unfair to give them a low grade in social studies content knowledge just because they lack the language skills to express that knowledge. On the other hand, if he gives them a higher grade, is that fair to the students who really earned the same higher grade? It's a real conundrum...

Mr. Elkind's situation raises some essential issues about assessment. At the core of these issues is this question: How can ESOL students demonstrate their mastery of subject matter without confusing that knowledge with knowledge of the English language? As Mr. Elkind discovered, using the same tests for all the students in the class is not the answer.

## ESSAY QUESTIONS, MULTIPLE-CHOICE QUESTIONS, AND LANGUAGE DEMAND

Teachers often write tests similar to those Mr. Elkind uses. And they encounter the same difficulties because the language demand of the tests simply exceeds their ESOL students' limits.

It is easy to see why English language learners have difficulty with the short essay format. Essay responses require not only content information (concepts and vocabulary) but also high level English writing skills.

The difficulty of the multiple-choice format is less easy to see. This type of question demands unusually high English language *reading* skills. Well-written multiple-choice questions require careful analysis of four or five options in order to choose the best answer. Options that are long or worded with subtle distinctions cause language confusion that prevents ESOL students' from demonstrating their content knowledge. To English language learners, a test of several pages of multiple-choice questions appears to be a formidable task.

1. The Battle of Antietam was important because
   - a) the South regained all of Virginia but Stonewall Jackson was killed
   - b) Confederate troops abandoned Kentucky and increased Grant's determination to win
   - c) Richmond was saved from capture and northern forces retreated
   - d) Confederate retreat gave Lincoln the occasion to issue the Emancipation Proclamation

2. The people known as "Copperheads" were
   - a) policemen exempt from fighting to maintain order in northern cities
   - b) miners from the North who formed a fighting unit in the Union Army
   - c) men who deserted shortly after being paid for enlisting in the Confederate Army
   - d) Democrats demanding an immediate armistice and peaceful settlement of the war

3. The North and South had different opinions about tariffs. Choose the statement that is true:
   - a) The North wanted high tariffs because it helped sell tobacco and cotton in foreign countries.
   - b) The South wanted high tariffs because it helped factories make better goods.
   - c) The North wanted high tariffs because it made the price of foreign goods higher.
   - d) The South wanted high tariffs because it was good for foreign trade.

**FIGURE 8.1 Typical Multiple Choice Questions on the American Civil War**

So we return to the core question: how can ESOL students be tested in ways that allow them to express what they know? The solution is to modify test techniques and to offer alternative assessment. Simple changes can make big differences in student performance on tests.

## MODIFYING TEST TECHNIQUES

### Change the Format

Did you know that multiple-choice tests are unique to the American school system? The majority of students from other countries have never seen this popular format before their arrival in the U.S. classroom. A multiple-choice test with questions like those in Figure 8.1 overwhelms them, not just by its high-level reading demand, but also by its total unfamiliarity. ESOL students would benefit greatly from changes in the format of these multiple-choice questions.

***Completion questions*** are the simplest and best modification of the multiple-choice format. Replacing the options with a blank space lowers the reading and language demand and allows English language learners to focus their efforts only on content. Look at the tremendous difference in reading demand when the format of the three questions in Figure 8.1 is changed to this:

1. The Battle of Antietam was important because

   _____ .

2. "Copperheads" were people who _____

   _____ .

3.  The North wanted _____(high or low?)
    tariffs because_____ .

Essay questions, too, can be streamlined for ESOL students by allowing them to use *visuals and graphics.* Instead of using sentences and paragraphs, they could express their knowledge through the use of graphic organizers, T-lists, sequenced pictures, labeled diagrams and maps, or any other adaptation of ideas presented in Chapter 6.

Another modification of the essay question is the *cloze* technique. This involves a passage, written by the teacher, from which key words or phrases have been left as blanks for the student to fill in. It is really an elaboration of the completion technique that tests knowledge of several related items in a larger fill-in-the-blank paragraph format.

### Change the Rules
Modify some of your regular rules for communication while testing. For example, allow the use of a *bilingual dictionary.* Encourage and *answer questions* from ESOL students that don't influence or give away content. If possible, you or a bilingual student could *translate the directions* for a complicated test into the students' native language. You might even consider *translating the questions* themselves.

Use *flexible timing* for testing your ESOL students. Think about dividing the test into several shorter sections and giving each section separately. Consider *shortening the test* by selecting only concepts of primary importance. In Figure 8.1, the second question is an example of the type of question that could easily be eliminated.

85

Consider changing the whole test or parts of it to an *individual oral exam* for your ESOL students. Oral language may be an easier modality for them to use to convey content information.

If individual oral testing doesn't seem feasible to you, consider *pairing* two students of equal ability. By working together, they may be able to complete certain more challenging sections of the exam.


## DON'T "TEST" AT ALL!

"Not testing at all" doesn't *really* mean exactly what it says. It means using alternative assessment techniques instead of, or as a complement to, more traditional forms of tests. It is a valid way of evaluating ESOL students' content knowledge.

### Use Portfolio Assessment

Portfolio assessment is one type of alternative assessment that has gained popularity among teachers and school administrators in recent years. Teachers generally work together with their students to determine selection standards and evaluation criteria[5].

Portfolios empower students by enabling them to choose the items that will be evaluated. Students can demonstrate mastery of content through a wider variety of measures than a paper and pencil test would allow. Students can document growth of language and content knowledge over a period of time. Portfolio assessment is an adaptable and valuable tool. Not only

---

[5] For those interested in learning more about developing and using portfolio assessment, see O'Malley and Valdez Pierce in the suggested readings section at the end of the book.

ESOL students, but *all* students, benefit from its use for assessment.

**Evaluate Learning Logs**

Like portfolios, learning logs and content journals can be used as a valid means of evaluation. For ESOL students who keep them on a regular basis, learning logs will show progress over time. Students may be extra motivated to work on their learning logs or content journals knowing that they are being used for assessment purposes.

**Use Self-Assessment and Peer-Assessment**

Self-assessment and peer-assessments are useful to supplement and complement other types of evaluation. Teachers can write individual *checklists* to reflect students' own feelings about their comprehension of text or topic, contributions to class or group work, or areas of improvement or lack thereof (Figures 8.2 and

| Textbook: Chapter 12 | Usually Not | Sometimes | Almost Always |
|---|---|---|---|
| I understood the reading. | | | |
| I highlighted the text. | | | |
| I used a dictionary. | | | |
| I worked with a friend. | | | |

**FIGURE 8.2 Self-Assessment Checklist I**

| Textbook: Chapter 12 | 🙁 | 😐 | 🙂 |
|---|---|---|---|
| I understood the reading. | | | |
| I highlighted the text. | | | |
| I used a dictionary. | | | |
| I worked with a friend. | | | |

**FIGURE 8.3 Self-Assessment Checklist II**

8.3). For additional information about students' own evaluations, teachers may want to add an extra column for student comments. A more individually expressive format for self- and peer- assessment involves completing a set of *open-ended questions*, as shown in Figure 8.4.

1.  The concepts I understood were _____.

2.  The concepts I didn't understand were _____.

3.  I think I improved in _____.

4.  I think I need more improvement in _____.

5.  I need special help with _____.

6.  The kind of help I need is _____.

**FIGURE 8.4 Open-ended Self-Assessment**

Teachers who use self- and peer-assessment on a regular basis (at the end of a week or a grading period or at the end of a unit) find that it helps to establish and maintain a line of communication with their ESOL students. Students' insightful input can often help teachers find more effective techniques and approaches to facilitate comprehension. Students feel empowered by contributing to their own evaluations. There aren't many assessment techniques as positive as this one.

## THE ISSUE OF GRADING

You will not share Mr. Elkind's grading dilemma when you modify your regular tests or use alternative means of assessment. Evaluation that combines the results of several different assessment techniques produces a well-balanced picture of what your English language learners know about content. And, if you have also been actively applying the strategies to modify other aspects of instruction, you will see that the "picture" is exciting and dynamic—one you, and your ESOL students, will view with pride and pleasure.

Return for the last time to Mr. Elkind's middle school social studies classroom. Turn back, if you will, to the very first scenario about Mr. Elkind in Chapter 1. Do you feel more comfortable offering him advice now to help him with the challenge of meeting the academic needs of the English language learners in his classes?

I hope so...and I hope that you include in your advice the need to focus on the total picture: a change in *just one thing* will not produce the result Mr. Elkind is looking for. That's why his good idea of attempting to involve his ESOL students in class discussions by asking them simple questions didn't work! Mr. Elkind needs to look at all aspects of instruction and incorporate many more strategies and techniques to reach his goal.

If you conscientiously choose and integrate the guidelines and suggestions presented in this text into your classroom, you will be amazed at the outcome. Whatever the combination of strategies and techniques you use to facilitate your ESOL students' comprehension of content, you are building their self-confidence and self-esteem by encouraging their success through meaningful learning. To you, their teacher, will go the credit for making these students successful participants in the academic environment that is such an important part of their daily life.

In this exciting and rewarding challenge, I wish you best of luck.

Jodi Reiss

# GLOSSARY OF ACRONYMS

| | |
|---|---|
| **BICS** | **Basic Interpersonal Communication Skills** |
| **CALP** | **Cognitive Academic Language Proficiency** |
| **EFL** | **English as a Foreign Language** |
| **ELL** | **English Language Learner** |
| **ESL** | **English as a Second Language** |
| **ESOL** | **English for Speakers of Other Languages** |
| **LEP** | **Limited English Proficient** |
| **NEP** | **Non-English Proficient** |
| **NNS** | **Non-native Speaker** |
| **NS** | **Native Speaker** |
| **PEP** | **Partially English Proficient** |
| **TESOL** | **Teaching English to Speakers of Other Languages** |

# SPECIAL NOTES FOR TEACHERS OF MATH

## Content Specific Issues

Teachers of math should be aware that there are a number of issues that may arise when teaching students from other countries. Here are the most common ones.

Foreign countries use different techniques for processing subtraction and division problems. Computational sequencing may vary as well. If these approaches work for the students, it is best to leave them in place. Ask students to demonstrate how they arrive at an answer. You and your students will be fascinated, and your ESOL students will earn some extra esteem and respect.

The system of notation of large numbers used in many foreign countries is the reverse of ours. Periods are used instead of commas to mark off hundreds in large numbers, while commas instead of periods mark off decimal places

| U.S Notation | Foreign Nation |
|---|---|
| 7,234,567 | 7,234,567 |
| 15.25 | 15,25 |

Additionally, the concept of *billion* varies from our use of billion as one thousand million. In some foreign countries, one billion is equal to one million, million.

95

Numbers are highly ingrained in students' native language. Counting in English is particularly difficult, even for those with fully developed English language skills. Reading large numbers correctly and understanding large numbers orally are skills that improve slowly with a great deal of practice.

Finally, it is important to remember that most of the world's countries use the metric system of measurement. Foreign students will be accustomed to measuring in meters, liters, kilograms, and kilometers. They again need practice to learn and become comfortable with the U.S. system of feet, quarts, pounds, and miles.

## SPECIAL NOTES FOR TEACHERS OF SCIENCE

### Content Specific Issues

Teachers of science should be aware that for students from other parts of the world, science might not be as "pure" as we think. Issues that may arise when teaching students from other countries are most often based on culture.

The concept of science and scientific beliefs may vary based on the cultural backgrounds of students from other countries. Certain ethnicities may have cultural traditions that lead them to hold conflicting views of what we accept as common scientific beliefs.

Students' cultures may also have certain taboos that affect the study of science. Such activities as dissecting animals and handling human bones may be forbidden.

Culture and cultural beliefs are deeply ingrained; they are not easily changed or discarded. It is important for science teachers to determine if any topic or process may create a cultural conflict that needs to be discussed and resolved in a sensitive manner.

# SUGGESTIONS FOR FURTHER READING

Cantoni-Harvey, G. (1987). *Content-Area Language Instruction: Approaches and Strategies.* Reading, MA: Addison-Wesley Publishing.

Explores the relationship between second language acquisition and the development of academic knowledge and skills at the elementary and secondary levels. Examines factors affecting minority students' progress and offers strategies, activities and materials for classroom use.

Chamot, A. U., and O'Malley, J.M. (1994). *The CALLA Handbook.* Reading, MA: Addison-Wesley Publishing.

Presents a complete program model aimed at developing the academic language skills necessary for upper elementary and secondary ESOL students to participate in mainstream classes. Explains in detail how to select content, teach appropriate academic language, and encourage use of effective learning strategies for students in all content areas.

Diaz-Rico, L.T. and Weed, K.Z. (1995). *The Crosscultural, Language, and Academic Development Handbook: A Complete K-12 Reference Guide.* Boston, MA: Allyn and Bacon.

Brings together theories, ideas, and resources for promoting cross-cultural awareness, language development, and academic progress in a comprehensive format written for the regular classroom teacher.

Echevarria, J., and Graves, A. (1998). *Sheltered Content Instruction: Teaching English Language Learners with Diverse Abilities.* Boston, MA: Allyn and Bacon.

Offers in-depth information on methods for adapting instruction and curriculum across grade levels and subject areas for English language learners. Includes sections on learning strategies, curriculum adaptation, and adjusting discourse for more effective learning.

Fromkin, V. and Rodman, R. (1993). *An Introduction To Language (5$^{th}$ ed.).* Fort Worth, TX: Harcourt Brace Jovanovitch.

Presents basic concepts and ideas about language that assume no previous knowledge on the part of the reader. This user-friendly, clearly written text examines the nature of human language, grammatical, social, and biological aspects of language, and language in the computer age.

Genesee, F. and Upshur, J.A. (1996). *Classroom-Based Evaluation in Second Language Education.* New York: Cambridge University Press.

Emphasizes the value of classroom-based assessment as a tool for improving both teaching and learning. Includes detailed information about evaluating without tests (observations, portfolios, journals), with teacher-made tests, and with standardized tests.

O'Malley, J. M. and Valdez Pierce, L. (1996). *Authentic Assessment for English Language Learners: Practical Approaches for Teachers.* Reading, MA: Addison-Wesley.

Provides effective strategies for assessing oral language, reading, writing, and the content areas, as well as practical approaches for using portfolios, self-assessment, and peer assessment. Includes guidelines for grading practices and reproducible checklists, scales, and rubrics. Also describes numerous classroom-based instructional activities usable as assessment techniques.

Oxford, R. L. (1990). *Language learning strategies: What every teacher should know.* Boston, MA: Heinle & Heinle.
Presents detailed ideas and recommendations for developing learning strategies in each of the four language skills with suggestions for integration into content area studies.

Richard-Amato, P.A. and Snow, M.A. (eds.). (1992). *The Multicultural Classroom: Readings for Content-Area Teachers.* Reading, MA: Addison-Wesley Publishing.
Presents selections from the works of experienced teachers and researchers that discuss content-specific instructional theories, practices, strategies, and materials for the classroom.

Scarcella, R. (1990). *Teaching Language Minority Students in the Multicultural Classroom.* Upper Saddle River, NJ: Prentice Hall Regents.
Provides practical suggestions for a culturally responsive classroom that promotes students' language development and content learning. Discusses issues affecting language minority students' progress in school, including effective communication, comprehensible lessons, fair assessments, and parent involvement.

Snow, M.A. and Brinton, D.B. (eds.) (1997). *The Content-Based Classroom: Perspectives on Integrating Language and Content.* White Plains, NY: Longman.
Examines practical models for teacher preparation and classroom strategies to apply the tenets of a content-based approach to language instruction.